(F)

IN

Science

THE BEST TEST PAPER BLUNDERS

Richard Benson

summersdale

F IN SCIENCE

Summersdale Publishers Ltd
46 West Street
Chichester
West Sussex
PO19 1RP
UK

www.summersdale.com

Printed and bound by CPI Group (UK) Ltd, Croydon, CR0 4YY

ISBN: 978-1-84953-323-2

Substantial discounts on bulk quantities of Summersdale books are available to corporations, professional associations and other organisations. For details telephone Summersdale Publishers on (+44-1243-771107), fax (+44-1243-786300) or email (nicky@summersdale.com).

Contents

Introduction..............................5

The Natural World...................7

Chemistry...............................22

Physics....................................37

Human Biology.......................52

Science and the Home............66

Introduction

Does thinking about Science exams bring up confusing memories of currents and currants, igneous rock and iguanas? Thousands of people have relived their exam-day nightmares with *F in Exams*, and we just couldn't resist bringing you some more hilarious test paper blunders in this bite-size Science edition.

This book is full to the brim with funny answers from clueless but canny students of science which will have you chuckling over chemistry, howling at human biology and in peals of laughter over physics! Just don't blame us if your science teacher tells you to come back when you're more evolved...

Subject: **The Natural World**

Different living organisms reproduce in different ways. Describe two methods of reproduction.

The Stork and Angel Gabriel

What is meant by microorganism?

A very small keyboard

How does the process of natural selection work?

The two captains just have to go with their instincts to pick their teams.

What is a genetically modified organism?

Something like a wig which has been made to make a bald person look like they have hair.

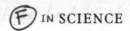

What are the properties of crude oil?

It's rude and has no manners.

What are the negative effects of global dimming?

Everybody gets thicker

What are the effects of rearing cattle?

Getting kicked in the teeth.

A phototropism involves a reaction to...

Having your picture taken (near the Equator)

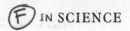

Explain the process of evolution.

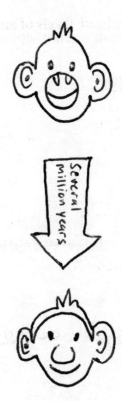

How do lichens indicate levels of air pollution?

semaphore

What is likely to happen to an individual that is poorly suited to its environment?

Be bought a new suit

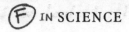

Why are white peppered moths likely to be more common than black ones in country areas?

Racism.

Why was Lamarck's theory of evolution discredited?

Because no one knew who he was.

What causes tectonic plates to move?

Noisy neighbours.

Which is the most abundant gas in the atmosphere?

farts.

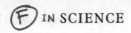

Why are coal, oil and natural gas non-renewable resources?

Because they always move on once their contract is up.

What is meant by the term 'biodiversity'?

IT'S A DOUBLE UNIVERSITY

Describe the properties of a meteor.

An animal that only eats meat.

The island of Madagascar houses many species that are not found anywhere else on the planet. Give one possible explanation for this.

Why would they Move? Madagascar is ace!

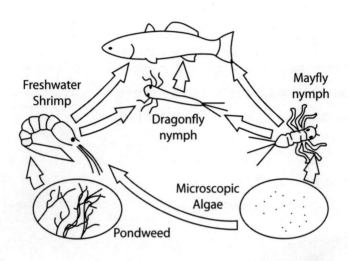

Freshwater Shrimp

Dragonfly nymph

Mayfly nymph

Microscopic Algae

Pondweed

In this food web, what is represented by the arrows?

Who fancies who.

There has been a marked rise in the percentage of carbon dioxide in the Earth's atmosphere over the last 50 years; suggest one reason for this.

Breathing.

Frog numbers are falling rapidly. Explain the effect this will have on the insect population.

They will have a party.

What is chlorophyll?

An ingredient in expensive shampoo.

Explain the process of eutrophication.

It's when a country joins the Euro.

Describe the purpose of cytoplasm.

In Ghostbusters II it was used
to make the Statue of Liberty
come to life. I've never seen
it used since.

What is the purpose of amylase?

It lets people called
Amy relax.

Subject: ....Chemistry...................

What is the unit 'Calorie' used to measure?

How much somebody will complain about their weight.

Describe a neutrino.

The opposite of an oldtrino.

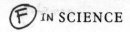
Define an alloy.

The fancy bit on a car wheel.

What is a polymer?

A group of mermaids.

What is the purpose of chromatography?

To take pictures of time.

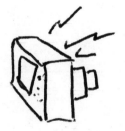

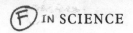
Describe two types of 'smart' material.

Fish and fruit help make you smart.

What nutrient is known for helping to produce healthy bones and teeth?

Bread crusts
(that's what my granny says)

What would be the best way to neutralise the effects of acid rain?

Alkaseltzer.

An element has the electronic structure 2,8,4. Which group is it in?

Steps.

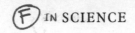

Explain the term 'half-life'.

When someone only goes out and
has fun half the time.

Describe a radioisotope.

A device for listening to the stars

Why is sodium stored under oil?

So it doesn't have as far to fall if you knock the packet over.

What happens to iron oxide in a blast furnace?

It gets hot

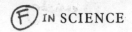

What does an ionic bond involve?

AN ION AND AN IRONING BOARD

What does a covalent bond involve?

a secret friendship between nuns

What does phytomining involve?

Mines and a boxing ring.

In comparison with large hydrocarbons, how would you describe small hydrocarbons?

They are smaller.

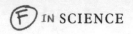
What process is used to purify copper?

Exorcism.

Why are potassium and sodium in the same group in the periodic table?

Because they are BFFs.

Where are vegetable oils found?

In the oils aisle.

What is mayonnaise an example of?

Salad dressing.

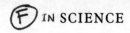

Define a super-saturated solution.

Water with extra water in it.

Give an example of an emulsion.

Dulux

What is the symbol for iron?

My Mum does this.

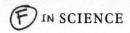

What is the purpose of a fractioning column?

A column with fractions
is useless, because it
wouldn't hold anything up.

What is an artificial pesticide?

Someone who is only pretending to be
annoying really.

Subject: **Physics**

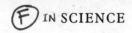

Why are catalytic converters fitted to cars?

To make sure no cats
get run over.

What is beta radiation?

Radiation that's nearly complete, but
needs to be tested.

What is a step-up transformer?

It's the sequel to Step Up and Transformers where the humans teach the robots to dance.

Explain how a vehicle can be designed to reduce friction.

It could secrete grease.

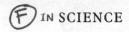

Draw the electronic component symbol for a switch.

Earth is closer to the Sun than Mars, and bigger. What are two other differences between the two planets?

1. Colour.
2. Aliens.

Explain the difference between a discrete variable and a categoric variable.

Discrete variables are quite secretive where as categoric variables are rather blunt.

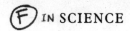

When conducting a study, what is the purpose of a control group?

To tell the others what to do.

Explain the process of thermal energy transfer.

Cuddles

Explain the difference between potential energy and useful energy.

Potential energy talks a lot but doesn't do much. Useful energy is less fun but more helpful.

What is the distance from the crest of one wave to the crest of the next wave called?

The sea.

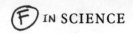

Describe the properties of a thermosoftening plastic.

It gets soft when you put it
in a flask with hot tea.

What is viscosity a measure of?

HOW SEE-THROUGH YOUR STRETCHY
CLOTHES ARE.

At the end of a marathon, a runner covers herself in a silvered space blanket. Explain how the space blanket helps keep the runner warm.

Alien technology.

Give one advantage, in any research project, of having a large sample size rather than a small sample size.

You can see it better.

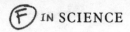

Van   Car

The diagram shows a van and a car. The two vehicles have the same mass and identical engines. Explain why the top speed of the car is greater than the top speed of the van.

It has go-faster stripes.

When taking an X-ray, why does the radiographer go behind a screen?

Privacy.

Explain the advantage of a CT scan compared to an X-ray.

It has more letters.

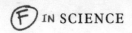

Explain how a transformer works.

It's a truck, then, it's a robot.

Name one key use of a plane mirror.

CHECK YOUR HAIR LOOKS GOOD AT THE END OF THE JOURNEY.

Explain the process of bioleaching.

It's when you choose natural bleach.

A student hears the sound waves produced by an ambulance siren. When the ambulance is stationary, the student hears a constant frequency. When the ambulance moves away from the student, the sound they hear changes. What is the name of this effect?

The doppleganger effect.

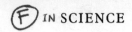
An astronomer uses a telescope to observe the movement of stars and planets. Give one advantage of having a telescope at the top of a high mountain rather than the bottom.

The mountain doesn't get in the way.

What is the key use for thermochromic plastic, and why?

To make cool stuff that changes colour.

What is the key use for memory metal, and why?

In guitar solos, to remember things

What is an electric current?

A zingy fruit.

Subject: **Human Biology**

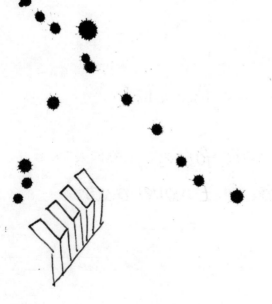

Describe the purpose of antibodies.

They are married to Uncle bodies

Name four diseases related to diet.

fatness, really fatness, when you're so fat you can't move, death.

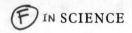

What changes take place in a girl during puberty?

SHE GETS BOOBS AND GETS STROPPY.

What is the meaning of the terms 'density dependent' and 'density independent'?

Density dependent is when you are thick and live at home. Density independent is when you are a bit less thick and live on your own.

Where in the human body is the Humerus found?

It changes because everyone's humerus is different.

Give an example of a disease caused by fungi.

Mushroomitis.

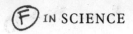

What is meant by the term 'placebo effect'?

TECHNICAL TERM FOR WHAT HAPPENS
WHEN PEOPLE GO 'EMO'.

What is the 'metabolic rate'?

Something that makes cake
eaters grow fat.

Describe the function of red blood cells.

To keep blood the right colour.

Describe the function of white blood cells.

Keeps white blood imprisoned.

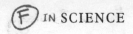

What is meant by immunity?

You can do bad things and get away with it.

What can vaccination involve?

Going to the beach, swimming, good food.

It is important to use antibiotics carefully because...

You'll run out of biotics.

What are the key differences between aerobic and anaerobic respiration?

'an'

What is a synapse?

A type of flying
dinosaur.

Give two similarities between an eye and a camera.

1. The round bit
2. They both blink.

Give one reason why MRSA is causing problems in hospitals.

Mr. Sa is always causing problems because he is rude and noisy.

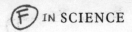

What is a fistula?

A mini fist

What is the purpose of plasma?

TVs

Before taking blood, a nurse dabs some alcohol onto the patient's arm. This makes the patient's skin feel cold.

Explain what happens to make the patient's skin feel cold.

A nurse dabs some alcohol onto the patient's arm.

Coronary heart disease is an illness affected by hereditary factors. Name two hereditary factors that affect our health.

Your mum's health and your dad's health.

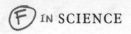

What causes spots?

Teenagers.

Your body needs to keep an internal temperature of 37°C. Name one way your body cools itself down if your temperature goes above 37°C.

TURNS THE HEATING DOWN

How are inherited factors passed from generation to generation?

By writing a will.

What is the purpose of bile?

When you want to show someone you're angry.

Subject: **Science and the Home**

Name three domestic sources of carbon dioxide.

1, Mum . 2, Dad . 3, Dog.

What is a pathogen?

Someone who doesn't believe in war.

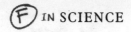

In 2006, building work began on the UK's largest wind farm at Whitelee in Scotland, consisting of 140 wind turbines with the capacity to generate enough electricity for 200,000 homes.

Give a key reason why this wind farm is unlikely to be able to satisfy the demands of 200,000 homes on a regular basis.

Because homes demand more than wind.

People are likely to object to the building of a wind farm because...

They want all the wind for themselves.

The Government is investing a lot of money in promoting energy-efficient products. This is because…

...they think this will make people like them.

What purpose is served by the national grid?

It helps when drawing maps.

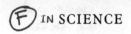

A study found that the use of energy-saving light bulbs actually meant a boiler requires more gas to heat a house.

The most likely explanation for this is that...

They LIED!

By 2020, it is projected that the amount of electricity generated from renewable sources will have doubled from 2005 levels.

The advantage of using more renewable sources of energy is...

People will stop complaining about global warming.

Explain two of the benefits of hydroelectric power
stations.

1) It keeps Hydra busy so
Hercules can do other things.

2) Hydra's heads grow back,
so it's a renewable energy
source.

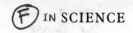

Explain the perceived risks of using Wi-fi.

If you're too enthusiastic at the tennis one you could slap your sister in the face.

Bioethanol is a biofuel. What does this mean?

Here is your answer!

Despite high fuel costs, it is still cheaper to generate electricity from fossil fuels or nuclear than it is from wind.

This is mainly because…

There are more dead things than wind.

Name a disadvantage of wind farms.

The smell.

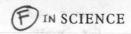

Suggest two reasons why it is an advantage to keep farm animals disease free.

Cows are really grumpy when they're ill and so are horses.

What is meant by the terms 'hard' and 'soft' water?

Hard water can beat up soft water

74

Nuclear power stations generate electricity without burning a fuel.

Name the process by which a nuclear fuel provides the energy needed to generate electricity.

Theft.

What is the advantage of nuclear fuels?

Accidents cause superpowers.

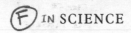
Research was carried out to determine whether there is a link between mobile phone usage and cancer. The £20 million funding for the research came partly from mobile phone companies. Give a reason why some people are concerned that the research was partly paid for by mobile phone companies.

Because they give terrible service.

Explain why the copper pipes inside a solar panel are painted black.

The engineers were big Rolling Stones fans

Smoking is known to be bad for your health. Give an
example of a smoking-related disease.

Coughing.

Suggest why the energy transferred by a television set
changes while you are watching it.

You change channel.

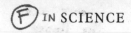

Some people worry that living close to electricity pylons might be bad for their health. Why might this be?

Because the people down the road near the pylon are weird.

It is important for our health to have a clean environment in our homes. Name two common pollutants in the home.

1. My brother
2. The dog

Give three common causes of energy loss in the home.

1. Comfy sofas.
2. Soap operas.
3. Mum's big dinners.

Why is it important to carry out a risk assessment before conducting an experiment?

So you know what's going to go wrong.

If you're interested in finding out more
about our books, find us on Facebook at
Summersdale Publishers
and follow us on Twitter at
@Summersdale.

www.summersdale.com